Olivia Mulligan

with love,
Liv
x

Fisher King Publishing

Copyright © Olivia Mulligan 2022

10:37

Paperback ISBN 978-1-914560-56-9
Hardback ISBN 978-1-914560-57-6
Digital ISBN 978-1-914560-58-3

Fisher King Publishing
www.fisherkingpublishing.co.uk

Mum, this one's for you.

'Olivia takes the minuscule and makes it magnificent.' *Harry Whittaker, BBC Radio York*

'Olivia Mulligan's 10:37 is a dive into a deep sea of personal, diverse and yet inclusive poetry. Here you will find that the everyday ordinary is full of intrigue, humour and surprise. A wonderful third collection.' *Patrick Green, Poet, Author of Sandpaper*

'I loved the wonderful celebration of life's mundane moments. A brilliant collection of clever poems, both light-hearted and layered.'
Emma Chapman, Author of How To Be A Good Wife

'Olivia writes with such purity, honesty and in the moment. Each poem tells a story, sets a scene and takes you somewhere visually. A stunning read. Something for everyone.'
Melody Reed, Singer/Songwriter

'10:37 will make you laugh out loud at times, nod your head vigorously or simply smile from ear to ear. I've found that poetry books I've read previously are often one dimensional - the author has a certain, safe style and their poems have a constant feel about them. 10:37 is pure genius and there is nothing at all one dimensional about Olivia's beautifully written book.'
Steve Phillip, Founder of The Jordan Legacy

'Olivia uses her skill of putting words to emotions, to create emotions from words. The simplest ideas are the most inspired, and 10:37 is Olivia at her creative best, connecting unrelated events like beads on a chain. Utterly absorbing.'
Chris Baily, Art in the Churches

**Each day, at 10:37am,
I wrote down what I heard.**

I did this project in secret, for 70 days.

Why? I wanted to create a different kind of
experiment to document my life's surroundings. I
came up with the idea for the project at 10:37am
and so it felt right to stick to this time each day.

I wanted to capture the weird, the wonderful and
the extraordinary in the ordinary.

Each day was the same time, the same world, but
a different feeling.

The snippets of the world at 10:37am are the
titles of each poem.

That's Just The Way It Is

Apologies, have we begun?
Do you want serious? Or a bit of fun?
How about word play? Do you want a pun?
Or a 'ball of fire' metaphor? (that's the sun)

Do you want freestyle or do you want rhyme?
I'll give you a long poem if you have time.
Looks like we're rhyming otherwise I'm –
Terribly sorry for assuming.

Apologies again. Now we have begun!
Do you want facts? Or do you want a tonne –
Of nonsense?

Do you want classical or modern life reflection?
Embracing the chaos and the imperfections?
Exploring the everyday human connection?
Expressing opinions with a different perception?

The glory of nature? Or the glory of Wifi?
Lyrical or narrative? Romantic or sci-fi?

It is what it is, so how can we agree?
How can we know what we all want to see?
It is what it is, so how about we be –
Ready for anything...

Here, boys!

I prefer the untouched
off-piste trails
with slippery roots
jungle-like corridors
crunchier leaves &
trees that haven't been seen
in a while

I prefer it here
alone
cradled by yellow
september sunlight
animated shadows
dancing like nobody is watching
nobody is watching
nobody is watching

nobody is judging
no thoughts are disturbing
no signposts are pointing
but her voice is calling

calling

calling from the footpath

The Crust

humans are spread
across the earth's crust
sprinkled amongst the stratosphere
absorbed by the atmosphere
sandwiched together in the world
gobbled up by the universe

I Told The Nurse About My Memory

life of reflections
reflecting
poetry
pausing
momentarily
forgotten
everything

everything
forgotten
momentarily
pausing
poetry
reflecting
reflections of life

Prices Have Gone Up By 74%

That's sixty eight pounds please
And yes, it's just a biscuit
I'm afraid that's the price
I'm afraid I can't fix it

I don't make up the prices, sir
I just work on the till
I understand your frustration, sir
But I can't adjust your bill

I would offer to pay half
And we could split the custard cream
I could end my shift early
Living the biscuit dream

But in reality I cannot help
I'm afraid it wouldn't be fair
My wage has recently decreased
And now I'm just paid thin air

So once again, that's sixty eight pounds please
Like you, I don't know why
It's one of those jokes that's not a joke
But if we don't laugh, we'll cry

If I Feel Like It

raindrops fall like voicemails
unanswered messages from the sky

please hold my hand from a distance
call me back
so we can try

hang out sometime
maybe

if it's not raining

Tonight

I think this is romance
A world of slow-moving-stillness
A dark world, lit up

I think this is romance
The city lights beneath us
Dressed in moonlight

I think this is romance
Gliding over rooftops
Unafraid of falling

I think this is romance
Motorway cars become glowworms
Floating down the stream

Yes, this is romance
Dancing through nightfall
Flying above the stars

It's An Hourly Rate

someone once asked me to describe time and without time for a breath without a single pause I told them that time is seconds minutes hours days years and years and years and years showing us that time is an ongoing story where the sun rises and the moon dances to the tick of the tick tock clock clocking hourly rates at work and working out to a stop watch and watching the big hand turn to meet the little hand and waiting for the next moment in time where we wait for a dentist appointment or hear the bell for school lunch it's time to wake up it's time to sleep it's time to walk it's time to run it's time to sing it's time to have a bath it's time for fireworks at new year it's time to meet a friend for a brew it's time to ask about a second date it's time to meet the family it's time to say I love you it's time to have a baby it's time to work out the due date it's the rate it takes a foetus to grow showing us the world has a debatable beginning and an unknown end an unknown end end end eventually creeping to the end we are edging to the end but the best part about time is when we forget about the end forget about the end forget about the end and time no longer exists

Thank You

Part I.
Formal (British)

Thank you, Sir
I appreciate your time
Thank you, thank you
For everything!
Truly, deeply, I'm –
Ever so grateful.

Part II
Informal (British)

Hiya
Y'alright?
Y'alright?
Nah.
Sup mate?
Nowt really.
Well, take care.
Ta.

Part III
Text

Thank u 4 today m8
I. O. U !!!
Hope 2 c u soon
Send my <3 2 Sue

PART IV
International

Gracias
Danke
I'd like to thank you...
Asante
Salamat
Merci beaucoup!
Grazie
Kiitos
Terima kasih
Mahalo
Tak
Cheers to you, from me!

That's My Grandad

He looks a little different without her
His green eyes have faded to grey
"I don't want you feeling sorry for me.
I'm doing just fine," he'll say.

He turns up his hearing aid volume
To hear his favourite song
Humming to the café playlist
He orders tea for one.

"Why have you written a sad poem?
She wouldn't want me sad," he'll say.
"She'd want me to enjoy this life –
To live, to laugh each day."

"Why have you written a poem at all?
There's nothing special about me."
He sits to watch the world go by –
Sipping his cup of tea.

This wasn't meant to be a sad poem –
Just a poem about a man...
Reminiscing about his loved one
And how their love began...

He looks a little different without her
His green eyes have faded to grey
"I don't want you feeling sorry for me.
I'm doing just fine," he'll say.

Take Exit 23 On The Left

Hi, is this still available?
Or would you say it's unsaleable
Because it is so small?

And how much would it cost to post?
I live in Devon, near the coast
Hence, why I'm looking for a wetsuit.

I hear facebook messenger ping-ping sounds
I told her postage would be seven pounds
And then she gave me her measurements.

I'm five foot four, so not too tall...
Do you think it will fit, or does it run small?
I told her it was ridiculously tiny.

I then felt a little wrong, googling her name
But then she told me, she did the same –
We were both writers.

Forget the wetsuit. Tell me more.
An instant friendship – I'm out of the door –
Driving down to Devon.

Stop! U-turn! You crazy fool.
I turn back to the house, playing it cool –
Take care,
I hope you find another wetsuit x

It's Really Red

the visual perception property
doesn't mean much to me
the spectrum of light
dancing with the eye
the colour, the colour I see

how do I describe red
the red poppies chanting blood
fire engine red
strawberry jam red
cliché love heart love

how do I describe blue
turning once red lips to ice
blueberry blue
sapphire blue
handsome eyes that entice

how do I describe gold
crystal grains of sand
champagne gold
sunset gold
the gold that's in his hand

how do I describe green
so green it smells of green
broccoli green
traffic light green
the rolling hills I've seen

how do I describe black

when black sheets cradle the moon
black cat purr
black velvet dress
the night will be over soon

how do I describe colour
the colours of being alive
we see, we taste
the pain, the bliss,
we touch, we feel, we thrive

I'm Looking For It

It's funny how we lose things.
Is it? Is it though?
One moment we have it, then don't
Keep searching high and low!

You'll find it when you stop looking
Thanks Sherlock. Great advice.
Think where did you last put it?
Well if I'm being precise – I DON'T KNOW.

Have you checked in the dishwasher?
Your pockets, the fridge, the sink?
I'll keep my eyes peeled for you
I promise not to blink!

So, have you found it yet?
You've been searching around for ages
Perhaps we should conduct a plan?
Search the house in stages?

What are you even looking for?
MY KEYS. I scream. I shout.
But why do you need them now?
SO I CAN LOCK YOU OUT.

He's A Nice Guy

The nice guy CV
dotted with pleasant experiences
a do good attitude
likeable attributes
a considerable latitude in helping others
and a long list of testimonials
confirming: he's a nice guy

Why? Because, well,
look at him
with his charming warmth
kind words
gentle aura
non-judgmental eyes
his ambidextrous limbs
making you a cup of coffee with one hand
and helping a little old lady across the road with the
other

Look at him
with his long list of friends
the positivity that he sends
his smile that never ends
and his tired legs
from when he travelled to the end of the earth
for a stranger

I Dunno

Haikus confuse me
I don't think I understand
The simplicity

Construction Site

Dear Brain,
There is nothing wrong
With this body...
We are under construction
A work-in-progress
A never-ending-project
Building
Distributing
Strengthening
Building new cells
Distributing blood
Strengthening our skeleton scaffolding
Holding us
Together...
Building
Distributing
Strengthening
Our vehicle for life!
This precious body is meant to grow
This precious body would like you to know
It's time to feel alive

Did You Have Fun?

Fire
Up
Noise

Familiar
Unfamiliar
Nonsensical

Folk song
Ukulele
Notes

Flamenco dancing
Urchins
Napkins

Fossils
Universe
Ninja

Fat
Udon
Noodles

Feeling
Useless yet
Necessary

From
Underneath
Nanoplankton

Fantasy
Underworld
Narrative

Find
Uber
Nonsense

Find fun
Utter fun
Nothing but fun

Aeroplane

This is your pilot speaking
Welcome on board this... plane
Welcome on board this seven three something
To me they're all the same

It's 5pm local time
But who knows when we'll land
Who knows what will happen
If we get there that'd be grand

There are some exit doors somewhere
I think there's one by the wing
Seat belts are there if you want them
But they're really not my thing

This is a non-smoking flight
But who am I to judge?
I'm not on top form today
So if I fall asleep, gimme a nudge

So yes, this is your pilot speaking
My first time flying a plane
I hope you have a pleasant flight
I hope to see you again...

I'll Be With You In A Moment

Dear Reader
Reading quickly
Quickly forgetting
The forgotten

Dear Reader
Barely reading
Simply scrolling
The screen

Dear Reader
Reading nothing
No thing helping
Nothing

Dear Reader
Dearly scrolling
Rolling fingertips
Over blue light

Dear Scroller
Scrolling fingertips
& tip toeing towards
The exit screen

Dear Blank Screen
Where have you been?
Time to call a friend &
Speak

Dear Speaker

Speaking familiar
Childlike chuckles
Once again

Dear Friend
Friendly reminder
The world will feel kinder
When we speak

The Toilet Flush (part I)

How dare you own a bladder
How dare you leave this room
How dare you have a colon
How dare you have a womb

You may leave this meeting once
But do not ask again
It's not lady like to make a noise
So please, embrace the pain

How dare you have a body
How dare you 'need to go'
Please keep this a secret
We don't want them to know

We are human

Sorry

S
O
R
R
Y

Sir I'm sorry
Oh – I mean madam
Really sorry
Ridiculous mistake
You are obviously female

Short hair though
Of course that doesn't matter
Really cool
Really suits you
You look great

So please forgive me
Oh beautiful woman!
Really? You don't like being called beautiful?
Roger that
Yikes. I'll stop talking

S
O
R
R
Y

I Think About The Lawn

my poor old lawn, I could have sworn I had already
done the weeding
but the thistles are up with the buttercups
and the grass - that needs
reseeding

my poor old lawn, I could have sworn that I had given
you a trim
but with weeds galore I find it a chore
to know where I should
begin

my poor old lawn, I could have sworn I'd taken better
care of you
and I feel bad that you look so sad
but truth is I
don't have a clue

bet my poor old lawn wishes it had never been born,
to live in such a mess
but for goodness sake I don't own a rake
and my mower has done a
death

When I Get Better

The nights come early, getting dark too soon
Festering in thick shadows – feeling lost
In my own house, I'm hiding from the moon
The 5pm gloom and the winter frost

Perhaps it will feel different in the morn
You'll see the person that you used to know
Perhaps it will feel different when it's dawn
The 'new-day-new-me,' is my go-to show

Curtains up, the applause comes from the storm
Fierce thoughts are howling, I forget my lines
The overthinking then begins to form
Forgetting that the sunlight will soon shine

A rainbow smudge is smeared across the sky
Let's paint the storm and not get lost in why

In My Personal Life

the smile is the coral reef
the photogenic pearly teeth
& vibrant eyes

the heart is the turquoise lagoon
for you to bathe in the sunlight moon
of warmth

the brain is what we already know
the marine biology, the ebb & flow
of waves

but the unconscious mind is deep below
the unknown waters
we're afraid to go...

It's Going Well

New year new you
Is recipe for disaster
Don't be extreme
Just try to look after
Your family
Your friends
Your neighbours
Your self
Look after others
Look after your health
Eat
Drink
Move
Sleep
Dance
Cry
Laugh
Weep
Tell others you love them
Keep your friends close
Take your vitamins
(the recommended dose)
Incorporate flossing
Morning and night
Nap when you need to
If that's what feels right
When the clock strikes twelve
That's your time:
New year same you
You're perfectly fine

I Hope It's Not Me

Excuse me, can you smell that?
This is not animosity
But when did you last have a bath?
(just out of curiosity)

It doesn't smell like a person
But a beef and onion pie
Microwaved and steaming
And we're all wondering why

How? When? Who? What?
What could smell so wrong?
Such a stink, unable to think
What could smell so strong?

Is it you, or is it me?
The forgotten camembert
The gift of body odour
That nobody asked to share...

The Cat Flap

eyelids lift
the insomnia shift
the sleepless gift
at night

silence speaks
floorboards creak
dripping tap
cat flap snap
traffic hum
rumbling tum
next door's bark
dazzled by dark
the decaf lied
thoughts collide

eyelids lift
the insomnia shift
the sleepless gift
at night

The Toilet Flush (Part II)

In a rush, little push
Let's cough for noise confusion
Shush, flush – quiet please
They must never know

We are human

The Milk Steamer

The milk steamer hiss
The latte art kiss
She studied the world
In the café

The waitress is a writer
Observing table no. three
Noticing the cuppa tea dialect
Askin' for more sugars

The cashier is an artist
Sleepy from late night
Biro sketches
Doodling on receipts

The receptionist is a pianist
A concert of emails
Humming the melody
Working 9-5

That person is a person
Just another person
Just another human
Doing human things

The milk steamer hiss
The latte art kiss
She studied the world
In the café

Mi Maleta

Greet. Seat. Drive. Stop.
Greet. Seat. Drive. Stop.
Greet. Seat. Drive. Stop.
Sometimes I imagine *not stopping*...
Whizzing past them and their horizontal arm
A day to myself won't do any harm.
Zipping through the city, the motorway,
Driving through sunset, day after day.
The bus & I, without a route,
Cruising to cruise, wherever suits.
A vanishing road, the wheels turn to wings,
I fly through Autumn, Winter and Spring.
Through the clouds on this bus-now-plane
I'll pack mi maleta, I'm off to Spain!
Out of this country, I'll never stop
Out of this world, I've lost the plot.
Greet. Seat. Drive. Stop.
Greet. Seat. Drive. Stop.
Greet. Seat. Keep Driving...

Footsteps On A Woodland Floor

Step by step we begin to disconnect –
Phone switched off and the 'out of office' on;
Stride by stride we begin to reconnect –
Footsteps and our breathing become our song.

We speak to forest trees as if they know –
The twists and turns that shuffle through our minds;
The mountains whisper, edging us to go –
To run, to climb, to search for and to find...

To find out what our soul already knew –
Running freely to live without regret;
Like dark clouds shifting - soon we see the blue –
We run to disconnect to reconnect.

We're aiming to be aimless as we roam –
We run to feel escape and find our home.

Go For It

Poetry is something special
Poetry is unique
The huddle of words, waiting to be heard
We write, we read, we speak

Poetry is the untold story
Already on the tip of your tongue –
Get out of your head, what the world's already said
You're too stupid
You're too old
You're too young

You're too ugly
You're too beautiful
You're too rich
You're too poor
You're too different
You're not different enough
We're looking for something more...

But what you have is all that you need
You don't need anything else to show;
There is no master key to Poetry
So just write what you already know...

Waiting For You

waiting
waiting
waiting

the hole-in-the-wall libraries
are a safe space to wait (I think)
where typed up inky stories are kept warm

beige pages wait under creaking floorboards
as more chords of silence are heard
waiting for hands to touch the spine

I'm here
waiting for you
like a book waits for her reader

sleeping under a hood of dust
a place where word chemistry is misunderstood,
lost amongst best-sellers

I'm here
waiting for you

waiting
waiting
waiting

This Is It

there is a rope
a harness around my waist
my high-pitched breath, the sniff off death
i'm ready to taste the taste
of freedom

freely feeling the ultimate chase
freely feeling the internal race
i'm ready to tumble, free-fall through space
i'm ready to feel

alive

That's The Idea

There it is!
Grown from yesterday's trouble
Thoughts collide, then double
Amongst the rubble

There it is!
Huddled next to the doubt
About to escape
From a quiet tongue

Run. There it is!
Growing into unknown
Surprising shapes
Suffocating the room with

Silent air
Flooding the minds with
Music
For the first time

The Dripping Tap

kids on the street, they be like: hey
i just wanna hear bout the everyday
got 99 problems in this rap
got sticky front door, got a dripping tap
i need to wash up, need to take out the bin
got hairs on my nipple, got a spot on my chin
got an ongoing headache, got a UTI
channel 4 doesn't work and i don't know why
got too many emails, need to unsubscribe
this social media just ain't my vibe
got too many errands, but i don't care enough
haven't got enough space, but got too much stuff
bills are on the up, car due the MOT
i don't want to buy one, but i want one free
got a hole in my bucket, got a hole in my sock
got a hole in my head: i got writer's block!
got a problem with reachin' this 99
i'm trying to impress but i ain't got time!
you see, that's the problem, need more hours in the day
with more minutes in the hour i be like:
hey.
we got this.

Woah

Her name is November:
November Rainstorm;
Sister of November Sunshine,
Daughter of October Moonlight –
Mother of Today's Rainbow –
Making the world pause,
Losing their vocabulary
Saying nothing, but –
Woah.

Dear Customer, We Are Now Closing Till Number 4

I go in for potatoes, two pints of milk and bread
I exit with a dog bed and tools to cut my hedge

I don't even have a dog. Perhaps they sell those too?
I shoulder rub as I search, lost in the Aldi zoo

Forget the dog, my basket's full of all my favourite brands
I need another basket or another pair of hands

Wheetabix are Bixies, Shredded Wheat are now Wheat Shreds
Lurpack spread is Norpack spread, just to mess with your head

Head & Shoulders is now Head Strong, Fruit Shoots are Fruity Shots
This week's offer is hiking gear so I decide to buy the lot

My cart is full of affordable wine and a brand new six man tent
A year's supply of cleaning products, I now have the Aldi scent

You see, I've worked up quite a sweat, bag packing at top speed
The cashier attack, my bruises black, my nose begins to bleed

Janet, on till number three, she didn't mean any harm

But her check out speed knocks me out with her
powerful underarm

The tin of beans comes hurtling, SMACK into my head
I exit with my war wounds and forgot my milk and bread

Don't You Want Me Baby

Firstly, the dishwasher. Please don't load it like that.
Secondly, the delivery addiction. We don't need any more tat.
Thirdly, the snoring. I've forgotten how it feels to sleep.
Fourthly, the vegan debate. Yes, I know it's a sheep.
Fifthly, the butter knife. Use a clean one for the jam.
Sixthly, it's 'family' not the famalam!
Seventhly, the volume. Why is your voice so loud?
Eighthly, the burping. Does it make you proud?
Ninethly, is that even a word? This list is far too long.
Tenthly, please don't sing, if you don't know the words to the song.
Eleventhly, the emojis. Why do you use so many?
Twelthly, your spending habits. We're trying to save the pennies.
Thirteenthly, the toilet seat. How many times do you need to be told?
Finally, don't call me baby. I'm 27 years old.

Secrecy

he tried to cry
alone in the dark
but the street-lamps
lit up his face

he tried to cry
eyelids down
the guilty teardrops
chase

other teardrops
falling off-piste
down hot cheeks
on show

with nowhere to go
the secret crying
stops
perhaps they'll never know

11 Minutes

it takes 11 minutes to unload the dishwasher
it takes 11 minutes to telephone a friend
it takes 11 minutes to download the latest software
it takes 11 minutes to overcook hard boiled eggs
it takes 11 minutes to fold the laundry
it takes 11 minutes to water the plants
it takes 11 minutes to read a bedtime story
it takes 11 minutes to feed the ducks
it takes 11 minutes to walk to the bus stop
it takes 11 minutes to drive from Dishforth to Boroughbridge
it takes 11 minutes to stand in the queue at the post office
it takes 11 minutes to listen to your favourite song three times
it takes 11 minutes to drink a cup of tea
it takes 11 minutes to ponder in silence
it takes 11 minutes to watch the sunset
it takes 11 minutes to drift off to sleep
it takes 11 minutes to dance around the kitchen
it takes 11 minutes to celebrate you're a billionaire
it takes 11 minutes to do a tv interview
it takes 11 minutes to fly to the moon

With Ice

Step into the rink
The blank white canvas
For a moment think:
Will they understand us?

Wait for the melody
Let inspiration come
The movement remedy
The dance has begun

Perfection on ice
A lifetime of spins
To glide and slice
The fire within

The world doesn't know
The previous falls
They're here for the show
The audience applause

The exterior bliss
The sequined capes
Entranced by this
Language of shapes

A story is told
A routine so precise
Performing for gold
Poetry on ice

From A Different Country

in this strange city
perhaps the pigeons will be my friends
cooing a foreign language
they agree it is cold

in this strange city
perhaps the loneliness will end
I'll practice my own language
I'm too young to feel old

in this strange city
perhaps my heart will mend
someone will speak my language
our story will unfold

One With Bacon

One with Bacon!
One with veg!
Poor little piglet.
Poor little hedge.
Spicy sausage
Or plastic cheese
Have your sarnie
However you please!
Ham or lettuce
And by that I mean
Sarnie with oink
Or sarnie with greens.
Hummus or beef
Chickpea or cow
You do you
And you do it how
You like it.

Unwanted Cough

internal gutter
throat cutter
lungs flutter
stut-stut-stutter
phlegmy butter
chesty splutter
coughing nutter
strangers mutter
tut-tut tutters
"PLEASE
shut her up!"

My Own Thoughts

without blinking
moments shrinking
gave up thinking
eyes would sparkle again

no words to say
in daylight day
a darkness lay
in my head

a silent war
cold to the core
ongoing chore
ongoing dread

the young bones creak
but if I speak
will I seem weak
to you?

the friendship call
caught my fall
love conquers all
it's true

in just one year
a thousand tears
fighting fears
for you

for me

to be
so free
I see

I feel, I feel again

Saturday Night's Drunken Dreams

A deep sleep dream is where I sometimes write
A rhyme or rhythm prompts me to awake
Wide eyed I scribble by my bedside light
My dreamt up verse I cannot seem to shake

I dreamt that I was dreaming in a dream
A world where footsteps wandered with the rain
A midnight dream that delicately seems
To wander without fear through harsh terrain

I whispered to the words under my breath
A cosy chill caressed my sleeping spine
Floating free from the frozen icy depths
I'm diving to a place my words can shine

My dreams are vivid and my slumber deep
Last night I wrote this poem in my sleep

They're Rubbish

If it doesn't rhyme
I certainly won't like it.
I hate haikus too.

Have You Read The Reviews?

Dear two star reviewer,
Thank you for your rating.
Thank you for purchasing
And then proudly stating: you hate books.
I hate every book
Especially books that rhyme.
Well, two star reviewer
Looks like I've got time: to write a poem just for you.
Dear two star reviewer
Thank you for targeting me
Thanks to you I am now
A two star reviewee.

Rain

here it comes again
unwanted heavy rainfall
teardrops from your sky

you've been here before
painting puddles on your street
inspired by your clouds

stop to taste the rain
it will have a certain scent
reminding you that

it is meant to be

People Don't Move Quick Enough

tick off the to do list
compare mortgages and rentals
order weekly shop
cook with puy lentils

do a home workout
reply to Wendy
batch make Kombucha
meditate to be trendy

watch the news daily
absorb the headlines
update your status
respond to work deadlines

be in bed at nine
awake 'til twelve scrolling
seduced by blue light
information controlling

remember to breathe
breathe out your opinion
fit in but stand out
amongst the 8 billion

sort out your profile
try something new
there's 8 billion people
and then there is you

Spaghetti Bolognaise

One day we'll say
Those were the days
Those everyday days
The mundane maze, remember?

One day we'll say
Those were the days
That fashion craze
Wearing a beret or a poncho.

One day we'll say
Those were the days
A memoir haze
Felt like a phase, with you

One day we'll say
Those were the days
Our ordinary ways
Spaghetti bolognaise for dinner

One day we'll say
Those were the days
The indie cafes
The daily clichés, with you

Knockin' on the Dentist's Door

Covid has put a mask on me
We can't use the waiting room anymore
I hand sanitize for them to see
I knock again just to be sure

Knock knock knockin' on the dentist's door
Knock knock knockin' on the dentist's door
Knock knock knockin' on the dentist's door
Knock knock knockin' on the dentist's door

Halloween Princess

(co-written with 6 – 9 year olds in my Halloween poetry workshop)

Sleep in a coffin surrounded by bats,
Wear your cloaks from the skin of rats.
Plait beetles and worms into your hair,
Shout: *wahahaha, don't you dare!*
Gobble-gobble frogs legs for your lunch,
Human meat for supper, munch, munch, munch!
Live in a ghost ship or a haunted house,
Infected by rodents, the black cat, the mouse.
Swim in lava, drink spider's milk,
Make your capes from tarantula's silk.
Tiger's teeth in the potion unleashes:
Frightening people into a thousand pieces...

Very Annoying

creeping, peeping through yesterday's clouds
weeping a UV Ray mist
seeping through with a hot glow
and oh
hello
i'm sunburnt.
pass the aloe vera.
what's that?
i can't hear ya.
the birdsong is too loud
so speak up.
no.
be quiet.
i'm relaxing.
i'm relaxing with audio book files, watermelon smiles &
an iced cold can
that's lukewarm.
relaxing with the sweat and the sunburnt toes
relaxing with the streaming eyes and the itchy nose
relaxing with the mosquitos and the wasp that's acting
shifty
relaxing with the 99 that's cost me £3.50

Avo & Eggs

(When somebody asks me what I recommend from the all day brunch menu...)

To dip or not to dip?
That is the question...
Questioning dunkability
The possibility behind the shell
Telling a free range story
Anticipating those buttery wholegrain soldiers

To flip or not to flip?
That is the question...
Sunnyside up or yolk face down
Drowning in yolk porn regardless
Awaiting the avocado companion
(or crispy bacon)
Eagerly begging to be gobbled
Cobbled together with love, salt & pepper...

Fancy eggs? That we can do –
Duck eggs, quail eggs, geese eggs too
Or something sweet? Is that up your street?
Crepes with fruit compote for a brunchy treat –
We crack, we break, we whisk, we bake
Chocolate, lemon or pistachio cake –
We dip, we flip, we poach & fry
On crumpets, white bloomer, gluten free or rye
We boil, we scramble, we omlette, we pickle
Adding herbs & chilli or whatever might tickle
Your fancy...

So let me know what you crave the most!

"Just a teacake or a slice of toast."

Team GB

Alexa. How do I become an Olympian?
I want to be the best of the best
How do I represent my country?
How can I wear that GB vest?

I'm sorry. I didn't quite get that.
I want to be at Tokyo 2021
Olympic trials for Tokyo:
That date has been and gone.

OK. What about 2024?
How do I start to train?
Train times from 20:24
Alexa, you've missed the point again.

I'm sorry, how can I help you?
Tell me what sport I should choose…
Here are the top 10 UK sports:
Drinking tea, waiting in queues

Alexa, stop! I want to be an Olympian
I want to wear that GB vest…
Temperature today is 21 degrees
A light cotton would be best.

Alexa, I give up.
It's as if you're taking the mick!
This is why you're not an Olympian
It seems you give up too quick.

Excuse me. I beg your pardon

I haven't given up on that vest!
As a friend, I think you should
Stick to what you know best.

My talents are rather useless
But my voice is rather loud...
I'll be the Olympics best supporter
Cheering them from the crowds.

I'm sorry I didn't quite get that.
Your voice is too quiet to hear.
That's it Alexa, I'm switching you off
Time for you to disappear.

Playing 'Disappear' by Beyonce
Actually, that's quite a good song.
Perhaps singing in my kitchen is what I do best
The Olympic sing along.

It's the Olympic kitchen dance!
The race from fridge to oven door!
Secretly plotting my Olympic debut
At Paris 2024...

The Storm

A message from the sky
There is a voicemail for you
You have one new message
From what was once blue
Now grey now black
A midday darkness
Calling, calling
Calling, regardless, of the response.
Locking the doors
Closing the curtains
Calling, calling
The storm is certain, you will react.

Please leave your message
After the tone
The storm continues
To dance alone
Flooding the streets
With chaotic cries
The tantrum takes over
Possessions fly
From delicate hands
Lost in the gust
Exposed, exposed
Unable to trust.

Oh Dear

Swearing is poor vocabulary –
Have you heard that before?
Well, son of a monkey.
Shut the front door!

Oh sugar!
Oh fudge!
Oh son of a gun!
Holy cow!
Gee willickers!
What have you done?

Oh snap!
Gee whiz!
Crikey!
Dangnabbit!
Oh my gosh!
OMG!
Eat soap!
Dang rabbit!

For Pete's sake!
Fish paste!
Mother of pearl!
Pokemon!
Geez Louise!
(oh what a girl)

Jiminy Cricket!
Tartar sauce!
I don't give a Donald Duck!!!

But if the moment overtakes you
You're allowed to say oh
fiddlesticks.

The Luck Of The Draw

usually you win, being a king
I was just born a queen.
but the look on your face, when I won with my ace,
you really should have seen it coming.

It Won't Do Any Harm

get outside and go.
smile and say hello.
then ask: how are you?
cup of tea for two?
picnic under a tree.
dip toes in the sea.
soggy socks will dry.
hear the birdsong fly!
remember how to cheer.
laughter lines appear.
wander just to roam.
finally feel at home.
see the sunlight fade.
road-trip plans are made.
get outside and go.
otherwise you'll never know.

Follow Me

like
follow
share
as you run...
as you run...
as you run...

i run
he runs
she runs
they run
we run

as we run
it's more than a thumbs-up-like
(it's a love)
sharing our favourite trail routes &
replying to the mountains...

Tractor

Field
Mud
Barn
Cow
Gate
Fence
Tree
Oh I got a brand new combine harvester
Do you fancy a day out with me?
Field
Mud
Barn
Cow
Gate
Fence
Tree
Oh I got a brand new combine harvester
I'll give you a ride for free
Field
Mud
Barn
Cow
Gate
Fence
Tree
Oh I got a brand new combine harvester
But someone nicked my key

Crunching on Carrot Sticks & Hummus

Veganism is a sensitive topic
So I won't get too gory
But instead, a different approach:
It's called, 'The Chickpea story.'

Drowning in brine
Trapped in a tin
It seems life is over
Before it could begin

Roasted and blitzed
With lemon juice and dill
The cling film suffocation:
Left in the fridge to chill

A pulse without a pulse
A legume without a leg
But if a chickpea had a voice
That voice would surely beg
NO MORE HUMMUS!

Doo Doo Doo Doo Doo

Inspired to try and write poetry without any
vowels. It is very difficult.
nsprd t try nd wrt ptry wtht ny vwls. t s vry dffclt.

oi oi,
looking for

oodles of proof
bloodwork truth

cocooned amongst soft
vowels on our tongue

sung by u
A E I O U

a world without u
A E I O U

the words so few
a world without u

A E I O U
cannot be true

why try?
sync myths,
gypsy hymns,
why shyly cry thy shy rhythm?

I Need To Stretch My Calves

Mile one has been and gone
That was easy peasy.
Two, three, four, give me more
It's still feeling pretty breezy!
Five and six, I get my fix
But run a bit too fast...
Seven, eight, nine in record time
Now I don't think I'll last.
Calf starts nagging at mile 10,
I'm burping last night's curry.
My watch tells me to pick up the pace
But my legs don't want to hurry.
Mile 15 things go downhill...
Ironically we start to climb.
Just one foot in front of the other
Don't worry about the time.
Mile 18 is never ending –
Things then rapidly decline.
I genuinely think I'm going backwards...
I'm fine. I'm fine. I'm fine.
But who invented chaffing?
Who invented running at all?
Just 10 more little miles to go...
Am I allowed to crawl?
Mile 23 I start to see
The end is almost in sight!
Out of nowhere a second wind
A dig-deep-long run fight!
Well. That didn't last long
We're back to the stiff-leg-shuffle.
The sweat has drenched my headphones

And my podcast is a muffle.
Mile 28, I missed the gate
I just love getting lost!
Quads are rocks. Blood in socks.
Blistered toes are squashed.
Mile 29 is suspiciously fine
Just one more mile to go!
I feel like I've never run so hard
(but I've never run so slow)...
The final mile brings a smile –
A concoction of pride and pain.
I don't think I'm cut out for long runs
But I know I'll do it again.

Ferociously Typing

WARM UP YOUR FINGERTIPS
TRAIN LIKE A KEYBOARD WARRIOR
HEROICALLY HYDRATING
REFUELLING WITH COFFEE
REPEAT
REPEAT
REPEAT

PRACTISE PRIORITISING
MAKE MORE TIME
MAKE IT FLOW
MAKE IT RHYME
REPEAT
REPEAT
REPEAT

LEARN TO RUSH
BUT KEEP THINGS NEAT
DO MORE, BE MORE
PING, BUZZ, TWEET
REPEAT
REPEAT
REPEAT

LOOK AFTER YOUR INBOX
STAY GLUED TO YOUR SEAT
KEEP WORKING 'TIL LATE
DON'T STOP TO EAT
REPEAT
REPEAT
REPEAT

ADMIT DEFEAT

DO NOT REPEAT

REST!

The Committee

Let's make this a quick one.
We all have lives, you see.
Keep it brief. Alright Keith?
Who's up first? Oh, it's me!

Thank you all for being here.
There's not much to report.
Keep doing what you do.
Thanks for all your support.

"Not much to report?" said Tracy.
"What about the summer fair?
The race, the bake sale, the auction,
And discuss who on earth will chair

Next month's meeting when you're in Spain."
Portugal, I correct.
"The budget, the posters, the venue hire,"
"I have to interject..."

Keith pipes up from the back
"Things aren't looking good...
I spoke with Mary about the hall
And I think she misunderstood...."

Thirty five minutes later
After a word by word report
Tangent after tangent
Word vomit of his thoughts...

We learnt that Mary does pilates

On a Thursday morning at 10,
Which is why she didn't answer the phone
So he had to ring again.

Speaking of phones, his camera is broken,
So now he can't take pictures.
Speaking of phones, speaking of Mary
Berry's sponge cake mixtures.

Speaking of spoons, speaking of metal,
Speaking of last year's trophy,
Speaking of last year, speaking of Scarborough,
Speaking of a dental nurse called Sophie.

Speaking of Sophie, speaking of sofas,
Speaking of the sale at DFS,
Speaking of materials and allergic reactions,
Speaking of the rash that's on his chest.

Even I get caught up in the nonsense,
Suggesting aloe vera lotion...
Speaking of Vera, how is she doing?
What came of the commotion?

Did she ever return the plastic cones?
Or are we still one short?
My phone buzzes to send me an alert
MEETING OVER RUN. ABORT

Thanks everyone. Time to get home.
Thanks for your input, Keith.
Homework for next time, keep it up
But try to keep it brief!

We all have homes to get to
So let's work on our time limits
But, before we go, Tracy, dear,
Please add this to the minutes:

Rushed my dinner to get here –
To the village hall plastic seating.
Eighty three minutes I'll never get back.
Another pointless meeting.

Always Wary

wait – wait – wait –
I can't – I can't – I can't –
I can't wait for freedom
I can't wait to see you
I can't – I can't – I can't –

wait – wait – wait –
I can't – I can't – I can't –
I can't wait to see you
(without being near you)
I can't – I can't – I can't –

I want – I want – I want –
to see – to see – to see –
I do want to see you
without actually seeing you
because I don't know how to be

I want – I want – I want –
to see – to see – to see –
I want to want to see you
without actually seeing you
because today I don't feel like me

I'm Not Sure

I asked my mother to write a poem
She said *I don't know how*
I said not to overthink things
Just be in the here and now.
She said *I thought that was the point*
To deeply, deeply think
I said the hardest bit is starting
To put your thoughts to ink...
She said *I'm not too sure about this*
I don't think this is for me
I said how will you ever know?
If you don't have a go and see?
She said *what about the rhythm?*
The rhyme? The structure? The length?
I suggested she start with a title
She said Give Me Strength

Give me Strength: A poem by my Mother

Oh give me strength
With this unknown length

I can certainly see
This isn't for me

Running out of ink
Struggling to think

Right here, right now
I don't know how
To write a poem

Index

People' on BBC iPlayer)

ACKNOWLEDGEMENTS

I would like to thank Mum for her love and listening ear
Dad for his honesty after having a beer
James for his hugs and his cups of tea
Fisher King for publishing and believing in me
Harry Whittaker for his wonderful ongoing support
My friends for listening to my rambling thoughts
All you lovely people who bought this book
Finally, my cat, who doesn't give a monkeys.

ABOUT THE AUTHOR

Liv's first book of poetry, Poems On The Gate Post, was published in 2020. Since then, she has made sharing her poetry with others top of her to do list. Liv has taken to the stage performing her poetry, she runs regular poetry workshops for both children and adults and at the start of 2021, was appointed BBC Radio York's Poet Laureate. Also in 2021 Liv's second book of poetry, Advice from a Stranger, was published to wide acclaim.

Facebook: Olivia Mulligan Poetry
Instagram: Liv_Mulligan_Poet
Podcast on Spotify: Not Another Poem

Lightning Source UK Ltd.
Milton Keynes UK
UKHW021001221222
414275UK00010B/153

9 781914 560569